Wild Planet

Wild Planet

Explore amazing animals in their natural habitats

Bath · New York · Singapore · Hong Kong · Cologne · Delhi
Melbourne · Amsterdam · Johannesburg · Auckland · Shenzhen

First published by Parragon in 2010

Parragon
Queen Street House
4 Queen Street
Bath BA1 1HE, UK

Designed, produced and packaged by
Stonecastle Graphics Limited

Designed by Sue Pressley and Paul Turner
Edited by Philip de Ste. Croix

ISBN 978-1-4454-2005-9

Printed in China

Page 1: A female polar bear and cub walking across Arctic ice.

Page 2: The majestic Siberian tiger is the largest of the big cats.

Page 3: A female rufous hummingbird feeds on nectar.

Right: Most of the world's squid (some 300 species) are able to change their skin colour to suit their surroundings.

Contents

Introduction

To the best of our knowledge, the Earth is the only place in the Universe which harbours life. And yet despite the seeming fragility of this tiny blue speck in the dark immensity of the cosmos, our planet simply teems with an incredible diversity of plants and animals. The numbers are truly mind-boggling. Scientists cannot say precisely how many plant and animal species inhabit the globe at present – many remain still to be discovered – but a rough estimate suggests between five million and 100 million!

This wonderfully illustrated book concentrates on some of the many remarkable animals that have evolved to colonize the watery depths, the many habitats in the terrestrial landscape and the airy realms above our heads. First we explore the marine and freshwater worlds which are populated both by incredible mammals, such as whales and seals, and the extraordinary diversity of fish species. We meet mighty predators, beautiful and colourful reef fish and some of the weirder creatures that occupy the watery environment that lies all around us.

Next we take wing – marvelling in the beauty and adaptability of the animals that have developed the power of flight. We encounter the sleek lethality of birds of prey as well as the extraordinary beauty of the fine feathers that adorn some of the most decorative animals in the world. Nor are flightless birds forgotten – ostriches, emus and penguins find their place here.

Then to the land where the cast list includes some of the most iconic mammals in creation: apes and monkeys, big cats, wolves, bears, giants like rhinos, hippos, elephants and giraffes, herd animals and forest dwellers. Finally the book turns to view two of the most ancient classes of animals that still survive on Earth – reptiles and amphibians. In all, it is a glorious celebration of some of the most fantastic of our fellow passengers aboard spaceship Earth.

Right: Herds of wildebeest are found in open and bush-covered savannah in south and east Africa, thriving in areas that are neither too wet nor too arid. The largest population is in the Serengeti, numbering over one million animals.

Water Creatures

Below: *Bottlenose dolphins are the most common and well-known species of all ocean dolphins, inhabiting temperate seas around the world. Females and young may live in groups (pods) of up to 100 individuals. They hunt together using echolocation to detect their prey. They will often drive a shoal of small fish round into a whirlpool towards the surface and then charge through the shoal to scoop up the fish until all are eaten.*

Left: *The green sea turtle inhabits both the Pacific and Atlantic oceans, spending most of its time in shallow coastal waters feeding on lush sea grasses. Females may return to the same beach where they were hatched to lay eggs in a hole which they dig with their flippers. When the hatchlings emerge, they instinctively head for the sea and must fend for themselves.*

Opposite: *Found in oceans around the world, the energetic humpback is a favourite of whale watchers. It feeds on krill and small fish which it often shepherds in a tightening circle before lunging with mouth wide agape to scoop up its prey.*

Above: The filter-feeding whale shark is the world's largest living fish, growing up to 12m (39ft) or more in length.

Left: The manta ray is the largest of the rays and specimens have been recorded that measure more than 7m (23ft) across.

Opposite: The eyes of a hammerhead shark are set at the edges of its hammer-shaped snout giving it 360-degree vision.

Below: Measuring up to 3m (10ft) long, the Caribbean reef shark is one of the largest apex predators in the reef ecosystem.

Right: Elephant seals derive their name from the large proboscis of the adult males (bulls) which resembles an elephant's trunk. It is used to produce extraordinarily loud roaring noises, especially during the mating season. These juvenile males are fighting to establish their territory.

Below: The walrus is found in the icy waters of the Arctic Ocean and is immediately recognized by its prominent tusks, long whiskers and great bulk – adult males can weigh up to 2000kg (4400lb). Their preferred diet is bivalve molluscs, especially clams, but they also feed on shrimps, crabs and sea cucumbers.

Above left: The Harp Seal is native to the northern Atlantic Ocean and adjacent parts of the Arctic Ocean. Adults have a black harp or wishbone-shaped marking on their backs.

Above: The common, or harbour, seal is the most wide-ranging of the pinnipeds (fin-footed mammals) with an estimated population of between 400,000 and 500,000 individuals.

Left: The endangered New Zealand sea lion breeds around the coast of New Zealand and its sub-Antarctic islands. Males grow to around 3.5m (11.5ft) in length and weigh up to 230kg (500lb).

Opposite: *Healthy coral reefs create ideal habitats for a wealth of colourful marine fish species. Coral is made of tiny animal organisms called polyps that deposit calcium carbonate around themselves as they grow. Although coral reefs occupy less than one per cent of the surface area of the world's oceans, they provide a home for 25 per cent of all marine fish species. As many as 6000–8000 different species may inhabit reef environments. Reef fish need to survive in the complex underwater landscapes of coral reefs. For this manoeuvrability is more important than speed, so coral reef fish have developed bodies which optimize their ability to dart and change direction.*

This page: *Reef fish display a huge variety of dazzling and sometimes bizarre colours and patterns. This is in marked contrast to open water fish which are usually countershaded (darker above than below) in silvery colours. The patterns have different functions and are sometimes used to camouflage fish against a particular background. Some predatory fish have evolved camouflage that allows them to lie in wait and ambush their prey as it swims past. Some eye-catching contrasting patterns are used to warn predators that the prey fish has venomous spines or poisonous flesh. Coloration can also be used to help species recognize one another during mating.*

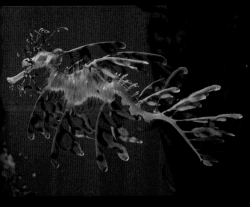

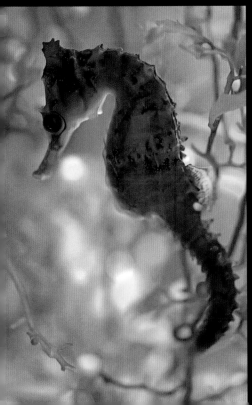

Above: Octopuses are invertebrates that live in rock crevices or coral reefs. They are able to squeeze into very small spaces where they lie in wait for prey such as crabs, molluscs and crayfish.

Left and above left: Over 30 different species of seahorse can be found in shallow tropical and temperate waters around the world. They swim rather slowly in a vertical position using fluttering motions of their dorsal and pectoral fins.

Right: The honeycomb moray eel has all-over camouflage – the pattern even extends to the inside of its mouth.

Above: Sea cucumbers are scavengers that feed on debris on the sea bed. They position themselves so that ocean currents carry food to them which they catch with their open tentacles.

Right: The semi-transparent, bell-shaped sea nettle is a carnivorous jellyfish. It immobilizes its prey with its stinging tentacles and then transfers the food to a central mouth cavity.
.

Below: There are over 1800 species of starfish found in the world's oceans. Most have five rays, or arms, which they use to propel themselves when hunting for molluscs and snails.

Above: The freshwater piranhas that live in the rivers of South America are notorious for their sharp teeth and voracious appetite for meat. All piranhas have a single row of sharp teeth in both jaws. They are tightly packed and interlocking making them ideal for the rapid puncture and shearing of flesh.

Above right: Cichlids, like this lyretail lamprologus, are members of a large family of freshwater fish that populate rivers and lakes in tropical regions. There are at least 1300 recorded species ranging in size from dwarf cichlids at 2.5cm (1in) to the largest Lake Tanganyikan cichlid at 1m (3ft) in length.

Right: Sockeye salmon are silvery-blue in colour while living in the Pacific Ocean, but prior to spawning both sexes turn red with green heads and sport a dark stripe on their sides. Males develop a hump on their back and the jaws become hooked during their return from the sea to the freshwater rivers where they spawn.

Opposite: Freshwater pike have the elongated, torpedo-like shape of most predatory fish, with pointed heads and sharp teeth. They can grow to a maximum recorded length of 1.8m (6ft), reaching a weight of around 35kg (77lb). They prey on smaller shoal fish and sometimes small mammals and birds.

Birds

This page: Birds of prey are found throughout the world. They hunt for food primarily on the wing, using their keen eyesight. Their talons and beaks tend to be relatively large, powerful and adapted for tearing flesh. Pictured here are a sparrowhawk (below), osprey (bottom) and jackal buzzard (right).

Opposite: The American bald eagle has a wingspan of up to 2.5m (98in) and an adult female may weigh up to 7kg (15lb).

Above: The barn owl is the most widely distributed species of owl, and one of the most widespread of all birds. However, it is rarely seen as it is a nocturnal hunter. It flies low, slow and silently over an area of open ground or farmland looking and listening for potential prey, such as voles, shrews and mice.

Opposite: The snowy owl is usually found in the northern circumpolar region where it makes its summer home, moving south in winter through Canada and northernmost Eurasia. Adult males are almost pure white. It feeds mainly on small rodents but will also prey on larger mammals and birds.

Above: The powerful Eurasian eagle owl has a wingspan of up to 200cm (80in) and measures up to 73cm (29in) in length. The owl's overall size, ear tufts and orange eyes make this bird visually very distinctive. It feeds mainly on small mammals, but can kill prey up to the size of foxes and young deer.

Left: Nightjars are medium-sized nocturnal birds with long wings, short legs and very short bills. They have acquired a mythic reputation as 'goatsuckers' from the mistaken belief that they suck milk from goats. They hunt at dusk and dawn, feeding mainly on moths and other large flying insects.

Right: The keel-billed toucan, also known as the sulphur-breasted toucan, is a brightly coloured South American bird with a huge bill. Its plumage is mainly black with a yellow neck and red feathers at the base of its tail. Its large colourful bill is around one-third the length of its overall body size. It lives in social groups in the canopies of tropical and subtropical forests where its diet consists mainly of a wide variety of fruit which it dissects neatly using its large bill to remove the stones. It roosts in holes in trees which are often lined with the stones from the fruit the birds have eaten. It is a poor flyer and moves mainly by hopping about from one branch to another.

Left: The Indian blue peafowl is the national bird of India. It is best known for the iridescent blue-green colours of the male's tail feathers which are raised and fanned in a spectacular display to attract the attention of the female peahen whose brown or grey coloration is dull in comparison.

Right: There are around 90 species of kingfisher around the world. All are similar in appearance with large heads, short tails and long, sharp, pointed beaks designed for fishing. They vary in colour but most are brightly coloured with little evident difference between the male and female plumage.

Left: The lilac-breasted roller is found in open woodland in sub-Saharan Africa. It perches at the tops of trees where it can best spot the movement of prey like insects and small lizards.

Right: The northern cardinal is a songbird found in woodlands, swamps and gardens in North America. The males are bright red with a distinctive crest, while the females are red-brown.

Below: Young lesser flamingos are born with grey plumage, but adults range from light pink to bright red due to the action of organic pigments present in their diet of shrimps and plankton.

Right: *The emu is the largest bird native to Australia and the second-largest bird in the world by height (up to 2m/6.5ft), after its relative the ostrich. Able to sprint at up to 50kph (30mph), these soft-feathered, flightless birds are nomadic and may travel long distances to feed on plants and insects.*

Opposite: *The flightless ostrich, native to Africa, is the world's largest bird, with an adult usually weighing up to 130kg (290lb) and with its head up to 2.8m (9ft) above the ground. It is able to run at speeds of up to 70kph (45mph). It mainly feeds on seeds, shrubs, grass, fruit, flowers and small insects.*

Above: *Most species of bee-eater are found in Africa but others occur in southern Europe, Australia and New Guinea. These tiny birds predominantly prey on flying insects, especially bees and wasps, which are caught in the air and eaten after the sting has been removed by banging the insect on a hard surface.*

Right: *Hummingbirds are among the smallest of birds. They are able to hover in mid-air by rapidly flapping their wings up to 90 times per second. They can even fly backwards, and are the only group of birds able to do so. Hummingbirds drink up to five times their own body weight in nectar each day.*

Right: African penguins are found on the southwestern coast of Africa, living in colonies on a number of islands between Namibia and Algoa Bay, near Port Elizabeth, South Africa. They grow up to 70cm (27in) tall and weigh up to 5kg (11lb). The pattern of chest stripe and spots is unique to every penguin.

Below: It is not uncommon for different penguin species to gather together in areas where prey is abundant. Here gentoos (left) share the safety of an Antarctic iceberg with chinstraps (right) in between hunting forays for krill and fish. Both species are preyed on by leopard seals and killer whales.

Above: *Rockhopper penguins are very appropriately named, as journeys from their nests in steep rocky gullies to the sea involve a fair amount of jumping over boulders and scree.*

Left: *Emperors are the most Antarctic penguins of all, breeding only on the ice sheet surrounding the continent itself. The female lays a single egg which is incubated solely by the male.*

Below: *King penguins form large colonies that may contain several thousand birds. Once the fluffy brown chicks are large enough, they gather together in crèches while the adults hunt.*

Left: The Arctic tern is strongly migratory, experiencing two summers each year as it migrates from its northern breeding grounds to the oceans around Antarctica and back, a round trip of about 71,000km (44,100 miles) each year. This is by far the longest regular migration undertaken by any animal.

Opposite: Puffins are easily recognized by their brightly striped beaks in the breeding season. They shed the colourful outer parts of their bills after breeding. They fly low over the ocean surface, diving to catch small fish, such as sandeels and herrings. They spend most of the year living far out at sea.

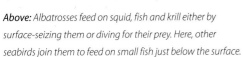

Above: Albatrosses feed on squid, fish and krill either by surface-seizing them or diving for their prey. Here, other seabirds join them to feed on small fish just below the surface.

Right: Common throughout the southern hemisphere, kelp gulls are opportunistic feeders, preying on and scavenging molluscs, fish, crustaceans and the eggs and chicks of other seabirds.

Below: Strikingly handsome cape gannets breed in large numbers on islands off the coast of southern Africa, with the largest colony of some 140,000 birds found on Malgas Island.

Land Mammals

Right: The squirrel monkey inhabits the tropical forests in Central and South America where it lives in large mixed groups high up in the forest canopy. Its diet consists mainly of fruit and insects.

Below: The vervet is one of the most common and widespread monkeys in Africa. It is typically found in grassland habitats and riverine forests bordering savannahs. They eat all the types of food that primates favour, especially fruit and flowers.

Below: Chimpanzees are members of the Hominidae family along with humans, gorillas and orang-utans. They are the closest living evolutionary relatives to humans. Chimpanzees are highly intelligent primates that inhabit the dense tropical rainforests and woodlands of central Africa where they eat a varied diet of fruit, nuts, seeds and insects. They live in large communities made up of separate family groups and each evening create individual 'sleeping nests' in the trees. They learn quickly, are able to use tools and can accomplish complex tasks involving problem-solving and dexterity. Sadly, increasing deforestation has made them an endangered species.

Above: Gorillas are the world's largest primates. A male gorilla can weigh up to 225kg (495lb) and stand 1.8m (6ft) tall. They are peaceful animals that live in close family groups of five to 30 individuals called troops. They travel together through the forest in search of leaves, vines and bamboo shoots to eat.

Right: Found only on the islands of Borneo and Sumatra, the orang-utan is the largest arboreal mammal in the world and is Asia's only great ape. The orang-utan lives a semi-solitary life high in the forest canopy, rarely descending to the forest floor. It is endangered and only about 60,000 remain in the wild.

Opposite: The cougar, also known as the mountain lion, puma or panther, is native to North America. These lone hunters range over territories stretching as far as 160km (100 miles) across. The cougar usually ambushes its varied prey which may be anything from a large moose or deer to a small mouse.

Right: The lynx can be found in high altitude forests with dense shrub cover in northern regions of Europe, Asia and North America. Characterized by tufts of hair on the ears and short tails, they are usually solitary animals. Lynxes hunt on the ground but can climb trees and even swim fast to catch fish.

Above: Tigers are amongst the most endangered animals on Earth. Native to Asia, today there are six sub-species of tiger, namely the Siberian, Bengal, Sumatran, Indochinese, Malayan and South China. Other sub-species are already extinct. The tiger's distinctive coat has over 100 stripes in a pattern which is unique to each individual. The stripes act as camouflage which helps the animal to conceal itself in the dappled shadows and long grass of its forest environment. Tigers typically hunt at night, feeding on large and medium-sized prey including water buffalo and deer, although they have also been known to kill elephant calves, bears and crocodiles.

Left: *Found on the wide open grasslands of Africa, the lion is the largest living cat after the tiger, with adult males weighing up to 250kg (550lb). Males are characterized by their distinctive manes which make them appear larger and more intimidating to rival males. Lions live in groups called prides which usually consist of one or two adult males, five or six related females and their offspring. The lionesses do most of the hunting and they stalk their chosen prey of wildebeest, impala, zebra, buffalo or warthogs in groups, before launching a fast coordinated attack. After the pride has gorged on the meal, they will sleep together in the shade for many hours.*

Above: *Due to loss of habitat and poaching, the leopard is now chiefly found only in sub-Saharan Africa. It survives due to its ability to adapt to different habitats and its opportunistic hunting behaviour. It can reach speeds of around 58kph (36mph) and carry a heavy prey carcass high up into the trees.*

Opposite: *The cheetah is capable of exceptional acceleration. It powers from 0 to 100kph (62mph) in three seconds, and reaches speeds of up to 120kph (75mph) in short bursts. It hunts early in the morning or in the cool of the evening, stalking its prey, mostly gazelle and impala, by sight rather than scent.*

Right: *Coyotes range from Alaska to Mexico and thrive in varied habitats from high altitude mountains to arid deserts. Expert hunters, they work in groups of two or three individuals, each taking it in turns to run after the prey while the others rest. When the prey is too tired to run further, the coyotes close in for the kill.*

Below: *African wild dogs are found on the open plains and sparse woodlands of sub-Saharan Africa. They are agile, long-legged canines with mottled coats and distinctive rounded ears. They live and hunt in social groups of around ten individuals preying mainly on various species of deer, antelope and zebra.*

Right: *The red fox is a largely nocturnal animal found in North America, Eurasia and Australia. Characterized by its prominent bushy tail, or 'brush', its dense coat varies in colour depending on its location and the time of year – from the familiar rusty red seen here to silver, grey and sometimes black.*

Opposite: *Arctic wolves inhabit the Canadian Arctic, Alaska and northern parts of Greenland where their thick white coats enable them to withstand sub-zero temperatures. They form small family groups to hunt caribou and other smaller prey. They fiercely defend their large territories against rival packs.*

Left: Brown bears live in the forests and mountains of North America, Europe and Asia. They live mainly solitary lives but may be seen in groups in Alaskan rivers during the summer when the salmon swim up river to spawn. The bears take fish constantly while food is plentiful in order to gain weight and lay down fat reserves before the coming winter. Adult bears can grow to 2.5m (8ft) in size and weigh 318kg (700lb).

Opposite: Sun bears are so named because of the bib-shaped patch on their chests. The smallest member of the bear family, they are very shy and live in the dense forests of southeast Asia.

Above: The black bear is North America's best-known and most common bear. Females are very protective of their young and these cubs will not have strayed far from their mother.

Right: Polar bears prey on seals which come up for air through holes in the Arctic ice. They are very strong swimmers and are insulated against the extreme cold by their thick pelts.

Below: Sloth bears are solitary animals which live in the forests of southeast Asia. Largely nocturnal, they feed on termites and ants, using long curved claws to dig them out of their nests.

Opposite: Female African savannah elephants live in highly structured family groups made up of various generations led by an older matriarch. As they mature, males adopt a solitary lifestyle before seeking a new herd where they may compete with other males for the right to breed with the females.

Right: Standing up to 5.2m (17ft) tall, giraffes are able to browse on leaves and twigs high up in acacia trees on the African grasslands. Herds of giraffe often mingle with other herbivores including zebra, wildebeest and antelope that benefit because giraffes can spot predators from a higher viewpoint.

Above: Despite its large size, the hippopotamus moves easily in water, swimming by kicking its back legs, or walking on the bottom. With small ears, eyes and nostrils set on the top of its head, it is well adapted to a semi-aquatic life and by closing its ears and nostrils it can stay under water for up to six minutes.

Opposite: White rhinoceroses live in herds of around 12 individuals on the grassy plains of Africa. Their broad, flat mouths enable them to chew large tufts of tough grass. White rhinos have two facial horns which are made of tough keratin, the same protein that forms hair, claws and fingernails.

Above: Hartebeest are grassland antelopes that live in herds of around 20 on the plains of Africa. Calves are born in the cover of tall grass but soon have to keep up with the rest of the herd.

Opposite: Impala are commonly found on African grasslands. Females and young may form herds of up to 200 individuals which stay on the move in search of food during dry seasons.

Below: The reindeer, or caribou, lives in large herds in the forests and tundra of the Arctic and sub-Arctic. Its thick coat has two layers which insulate it against very low temperatures.

Above: The red deer, found across most of Europe, is one of the largest deer species. The males, or stags, grow impressive antlers which they use in the 'rut' in the mating season when they compete with other males to breed with the females.

Following pages: The Serengeti in Africa hosts the world's largest overland annual migration of wildlife. Herds of over two million herbivores including wildebeest (left) and zebras (right) follow the rains in search of new grazing and water. During this hazardous round trip of about 3000km (1800 miles), they encounter difficult terrain and many predators.

Left: *The rare and elusive giant panda is an endangered species of bear that lives only in the remote mountainous regions of China in cool high-altitude forests. The giant panda can spend up to 10 or 12 hours a day feeding – its main food is bamboo which it consumes in great quantities, stripping the stalks with its powerful claws and crushing the tough bamboo with its large molar teeth and strong jaw muscles. Bamboo is not a particularly good source of nutrition but the advantage for the panda is that it is plentiful and available all the year round. Adults are solitary creatures but use their highly developed sense of smell to find each other during the mating season.*

Above: *The red panda lives in the temperate forests of the Himalayas where it survives on a diet consisting mainly of bamboo leaves and shoots. It is usually solitary and active from dusk to dawn, spending the day asleep. It sleeps stretched out on the branch of a tree with four legs dangling when it is hot, and curled up with its bushy tail over its face when it is cold.*

Opposite: *The nocturnal tarsier lives on the southern islands of the Philippines. It has huge eyes to help it see in the dark. The principal prey of this shy creature are large insects, which they can catch in flight, and even small birds and lizards.*

Left: *The Indian flying fox is a species of bat with a wingspan of up to 1.5m (5ft). It is so named because its head resembles that of a fox. It is found in tropical and subtropical forests in Asia where it feeds on nectar, blossom, pollen and fruit which it locates using its acute eyesight and keen sense of smell.*

Right: *The American red squirrel is a fiercely territorial animal found in forests where it feeds primarily on the seed cones of conifers. When food is plentiful, it stores some in a cache for winter consumption. In its territory, each squirrel builds several nests which are constructed of grass in the branches of trees.*

Above: *Lemurs are primates found only on the African island of Madagascar. The nocturnal grey mouse lemur inhabits dense forest where it feeds on fruit, flowers, nectar and insects. It stores fat in its tail but does not hibernate, although its activity levels do decline during winter when less food is available.*

Right: *Ring-tailed lemurs live in troops of around 18 individuals and are recognized by their distinctive black and white striped tails. They walk on the ground easily, but are most agile when moving through the trees where they forage for food. Their diet is mainly fruit but also includes leaves, tree bark and sap.*

Left: Porcupines are the third largest rodent in the world, after the capybara and the beaver. They have coats of sharp quills to deter predators. The quills are modified hairs covered in keratin and can be quickly shed so that they often stick in the skin of any attacker. Mostly nocturnal, they feed on grubs and plants.

Below: Beavers are found in North America and Eurasia where they are known for building dams in rivers and streams out of trees and branches, using their sharp teeth to cut down the wood. These dams create deep still water areas as protection against predators where the beavers build homes called lodges.

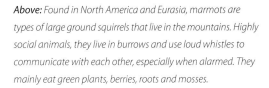

Above: Found in North America and Eurasia, marmots are types of large ground squirrels that live in the mountains. Highly social animals, they live in burrows and use loud whistles to communicate with each other, especially when alarmed. They mainly eat green plants, berries, roots and mosses.

Below: Echidnas, or spiny anteaters, are found in New Guinea and Australia. Covered with coarse hair and spines, they are similar to other spiny mammals such as hedgehogs and porcupines. Along with the platypus, they are the only mammals that lay eggs rather than give birth to live young.

Above: *Brants's whistling rat is found in tropical or subtropical dry shrubland and pastureland in Botswana, Namibia and South Africa. Its name derives from the whistle it makes when alarmed and which alerts others in its colony to the danger of a nearby predator, such as a bird of prey or snake.*

Above: *Hyraxes are small mammals resembling guinea pigs that are actually related to elephants and aardvarks. Though living species are only rabbit-sized, fossil remains indicate that hyraxes were once the size of oxen. In Africa today, hyraxes are 30cm (12in) at the shoulder and are found in diverse habitats from dry savannahs to dense rainforest. Living in colonies of around 50 individuals, family groups feed together on grasses, leaves, fruit, insects, birds' eggs and lizards.*

Right: *Field mice belong to a group of several species of broadly similar mice. They are mostly nocturnal, and live in woodlands, fields and hedgerows. Burrowing extensively, they dig a series of chambers and runs where they build nests and store food. Several adults and their young may live together in the same network of tunnels which will have at least two open entrances. They eat a range of seeds including acorns and sycamore seeds, as well as berries, worms and small insects.*

Reptiles and Amphibians

Right: The Yacare caiman is found in central South America. Around 10 million of these reptiles live in the Brazilian Pantanal wetlands, quite possibly the largest crocodilian population on Earth. They feed mainly on fish and birds.

Below: The fearsome saltwater crocodile is the largest of all living reptiles. Mature males can reach a length of 6m (20ft) or more and weigh in excess of 1300kg (2900lb).

Above: African Nile crocodiles feed on fish as well as larger mammals, such as waterbuck, warthogs, wildebeest and zebras. Opportunistic hunters, they lie mostly submerged and then rush forward to grab prey in their powerful jaws, dragging the victim into the water, and holding it underneath until it drowns.

Opposite: American alligators live in freshwater ponds, marshes, wetlands, rivers, lakes and swamps in the southeast United States. Large male alligators are solitary, territorial animals which can grow to 4.5m (15ft) in length and weigh 450kg (1000lb). Their diet is fish, turtles and small mammals.

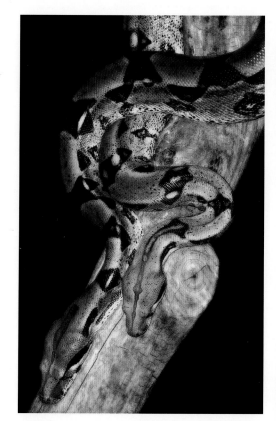

Left: The Madagascar tree boa is a non-venomous constrictor endemic to the island of Madagascar. Living in trees and generally nocturnal in habit, it feeds on bats and birds, using heat-receptive pits around its mouth to help it to locate its prey. Adults average between 1.2–1.5m (4–5ft) in length.

Below: Eastern racers are fast-moving diurnal snakes that are found in North America and down into Mexico. Their diet consists primarily of rodents, frogs and lizards, and some sub-species are known to climb trees in order to eat eggs and young birds. Smaller prey items are swallowed alive.

Above: Boa constrictors have highly variable and distinctively patterned skin which works as very effective camouflage in the jungles and forests of their natural range in Central and South America. They are large snakes and can reach lengths of anywhere from 1–4m (3–13ft).

Opposite: Young green tree pythons do not sport the bright green colours of adults, occurring in bright yellow, reddish and orange coloration instead. Adults average 1.2–2m (4–6.5ft) in length and live mostly in trees where they hunt. They use constriction to kill their prey of small mammals and reptiles.

Left: Tree-climbing snakes are incredibly adept at distributing their weight evenly. Many are so small and light that they can balance on the tiniest twigs, allowing them to silently approach and ambush small prey living among the leaves.

Below: Most of the world's snakes live on the ground and propel themselves by using serpentine movement, creating S-shapes with their flexible bodies to help them grip even the slightest irregularities in a smooth surface. This form of locomotion is extremely efficient and enables snakes to move quickly to chase prey or to avoid predators.

Above: When disturbed, most cobras can rear up and spread their neck (or hood) in a characteristic threat display. The Egyptian cobra (pictured), found in Africa, may grow to 2.4m (8ft) in length. Its bite delivers powerful venom which affects the nervous system, causing death by respiratory failure.

Opposite: The venomous Great Basin rattlesnake inhabits the hot dry southwestern states of the USA. The rattle at the end of the tail is composed of a series of nested, hollow beads which are actually modified scales from the tail tip. They make a sound when shaken as they beat against one another.

Left: The marine iguana, found only on the Galápagos Islands, has the ability, unique among modern lizards, to live and forage in the sea. It can dive to depths of 9m (30ft) in the ocean to feed on algae but can spend only a limited time in the cold water before returning to bask in the sun and warm up again.

Below: The red-headed rock agama is a lizard found in most of sub-Saharan Africa. In the breeding season the males develop very dramatic markings, the head and neck turning bright red and the body dark blue. Agamas are active during the day and scamper around catching insects on which they feed.

Above: The carnivorous Komodo dragon inhabits a group of small islands in Indonesia. A member of the monitor lizard family, it is the largest living species of lizard, growing to an average length of 2–3m (6.5–10ft) and weighing around 70kg (150lb). It feeds mainly on carrion but can ambush live prey.

Opposite: A tortoise in Africa's Kalahari desert. Like their marine cousins, the sea turtles, land-dwelling tortoises are shielded from predators by a thick protective shell into which they can retract their heads and limbs. Tortoises can vary in size from just a few centimetres to around 2m (6.5ft) in length.

Above: The eastern newt is a common salamander of eastern North America which lives in small lakes or ponds in damp forests. The striking orange-coloured juvenile stage, which occurs while the newt is land-dwelling, is known as a 'red eft'. Its skin secretes a poison when it is threatened or injured.

Below: Many species of chameleon possess a prehensile tail which helps them to hold on securely to branches as they move through undergrowth. The five toes on a chameleon's foot are fused into a group of two and a group of three, allowing them to grip tightly to narrow branches.

Above: The Madagascar day gecko lives in trees in the rainforests of the eastern coast of the African island of Madagascar, feeding on insects and nectar. This brightly coloured reptile is one of the largest living day geckos and can reach a total length of about 22cm (9in).

Left: Chameleons are distinguished by their separately mobile and stereoscopic eyes, their very long, highly modified tongues which they shoot out to catch prey, their swaying gait, often crests or horns on their distinctively shaped heads, and the ability of some to change colour as a means of camouflage.

Right: The common toad is widespread throughout Europe, with the exception of Ireland and some Mediterranean islands. Adult males usually grow to 8cm (3in) and adult females around 13cm (5in) and their skin ranges from green to brown in colour. They feed mainly on insects, slugs and worms.

Below: Brightly coloured poison dart frogs are native to Central and South America and, unlike most frogs, are active during the day. Their name derives from the fact that the indigenous Amerindian people use the toxic secretions from the frogs' skin to coat the tips of their blowpipe darts.

Above: Tree frogs are typically found in tall trees or other high-growing vegetation. They are tiny as their weight has to be borne by leaves and twigs. They do not normally descend to the ground, except to mate and spawn – some even build foam nests on leaves and rarely leave the trees at all.

Opposite: Consisting of more than 5000 species, frogs are among the most diverse groups of vertebrates. They range from tropic to sub-Arctic regions, although most are found in tropical rainforests. Due to their permeable skin, frogs are often semi-aquatic or inhabit wet areas, but they move easily on land.

Index

Picture credits

a = above, b = below, l = left, r = right, c = centre

© shutterstock.com

Lynsey Allan 55br; Konovalikov Andrey 15bc; Galyna Andrushko 36r, 44; Annetje 15al; ArvydasS 23bc; Brett Atkins 9; Kitch Bain 32br, 58bl; Paul Banton 43r; Craig Barhorst 26br; Andrew Barker 50ar; Thomas Barrat 1; Simone van den Berg 32ac; Mircea Bezergheanu 20cl, 51br; Nick Biemans 23al; Bob Blanchard 53; BogdanBoev 24br; S Borisov 40bl; P Borowka 14, 17bl; Brandelet 11; Joy Brown 26ar; Sascha Burkard 54; Rich Carey 10l, 10br, 16ar; capturephoto 49br; Alexander Chaikin 60–61c, 61r; Prasit Chansareekorn 25b; Alistair Cotton 52ar; Puchugin Dmitry 13bl; Dennis Donohoe 38a; Laura Dueliman 40ac; Brian Dunne 40 al; EcoPrint 6–7, 27, 45al, 51ar; Alex Edmonds 17r; Melinda Fawver 60al; Richard Fitzer 20bl; Susan Flashman 52bl; FloridaStock 21; Gentoo Multimedia Ltd 29l; Karen Givens 52bl; Andreas Gradin 45bl; Karen Hadley 32bl; Daniel Herbert 22; Niels Holm 8a; Sven Hoppe 31; Eric Isselée 33l, 42a, 46l, 46–47; Ivanova Inga 4–5; javarman 37; Andrejis Jegorovs 25al; kjersti Joergensen 16al; Jason Kasumovic 50bl; J Klingebiel 38br; Nadezhda V. Kulagina 8b; Eduard Kyslynskyy 35b; Hugh Lansdown 49al; Michael Ledray 55al; Keith Levit 36l; Francois Loubser 20r; Mark John Maclean 45ar; S. R. Maglione 34; David Mckee 15cl; Stephen Meese 13r; melissaf84 15ar, 16bl; Vladimir Melnik 13al; Holga Mette 49bl; Marek Mierzejewski 63; Hartmut Morgenthal 62ac; Sean Nel 38l; nialat 2; nouseforname 58al; Krzysztof Odziomek 19; Khoroshunova Olga 48l; Anna Omelchenko 43l; Alta Oosthulzen 30bl; Denis Pepin 39; Brad Phillips 56; pix2go 35a; Eduardo Rivero 24ar; Tony Rix 50al; rm 52ac; Sue Robinson 26al; Ron Rowan Photography 25ar, 49ar; schoor 18ar; Irakly Shanidze 41; Natalia Sinjushina & Evgenly Meyke 55ac; Radovan Spurny 33r; stormcab 16br; Tallllly 48r; Sarah Theophilus 62ar; David Thyberg 49c; Nikita Tiunov 17al; tubuceo 10 ar; ultimathule 24bl; VasikO 18br; Vatikaki 51al; Nicola Vernizzi 62bl; VikOl 12b; Stas Volik 23ar; Hans Welman 59; Shane White 50br; Peter Wollinga 42b; Michael Woodruff 3; worldswildlifewonders 12a; Vladimir Wrangel 18al.

© istockphoto.com

Daniel Brunner 57br; EcoPrint 30br; Andrew Howe 30ac; mikeuk 30al; MudGuy 28a; John Pitcher 57al; Patrick Roherty 29a, 29b; Lara Seregni 57ac; Rob Stegmann 60bl; Jose Tejo 29b; Peter Van Wagner 40br.